THE ORIGINAL LAWS OF CRICKET

FOREWORD BY MIKE ATHERTON

INTRODUCT  ...EL RUNDELL

Bodleian Library
UNIVERSITY OF OXFORD

First published in 2008 by the Bodleian Library
Broad Street, Oxford OX1 3BG

www.bodleianbookshop.co.uk

ISBN: 1 85124 312 7
ISBN 13: 978 1 85124 312 9

Foreword © Mike Atherton, 2008
Introduction and this edition © Bodleian Library, University of Oxford, 2008
Images pp. ii, 8, 26–7, 52 © Marylebone Cricket Club / Bridgeman Art Library, 2008
Images pp. 4, 11, 24, 29, 37, 41, 42–3, 44–5, 46–7, 48–9, 50, 53, 55, 58–9 © Marylebone Cricket Club, 2008
All other images © Bodleian Library, University of Oxford, 2008

Cover design by Dot Little
Internal design by JCS Publishing Services Ltd, www.jcs-publishing.co.uk
Printed in England by Cromwell Press Ltd, Trowbridge, Wilts.

A CIP record of this publication is available from the British Library

CONTENTS

Foreword..5

Introduction..9

The 1744 Code of the Laws of Cricket...................41

The 1755 Code of the Laws of Cricket..................51

The LAWS of the NOBLE GAME of CRICKET

as Established at the Star and Garter Pall-Mall by a Committee of Noblemen & Gentlemen.

THE BALL.

Must not weigh five ounces and a halfnor more than five ounces and three Quarters.

It cannot be changed during the Game, but with Consent of both Parties.

THE BAT.

Must not exceed Four Inches and One Quarter in the Widest Part 5.

THE STUMPS.

Must be Twenty two Inches, the Bail Six Inches long.

It is to have scuttled to win three Stumps instead of two to each Wicket, the Bail the same Length as above.

THE BOWLING CREASE.

Must be parrallel with the Stump, Three Feet in Length and a Return Crease.

THE POPPING CREASE.

Must be Three Feet Ten Inches from the Wicket, and the Wickets must be opposite to each other, at the Distance of Twenty two Yards.

THE PARTY

which goes from home.

Shall have the choice of the Innings, and the pitching of the Wickets, which shall be pitched within Thirty Yards of a Centre fixed by the Adversaries.

When the Parties meet at a Third Place the Bowlers shall toss up for the pitching of the first Wicket, and the Choice of going in.

THE BOWLER.

Must deliver the Ball with one Foot behind the Bowling Crease, and within the Return Crease, and shall bowl four Balls before he changes Wickets, which he shall do but once in the same Innings.

He may order the Player at his Wicket to stand on which Side of it he pleases.

THE STRIKER.

IS OUT,

If the Ball is bowled, off, or the Stump bowled out of the Ground, &c.

Or if the Ball from a stroke over or under his Bat or upon his Hands(but not Wrists) is held before it true that the Ground, though it be hugged to the Body of the Catcher.

Or if in striking, both his Feet are over the Popping Crease, and his Wicket is put down, excepting his Bat is grounded with in it.

Or if he runs out of his Ground to handle a Catch.

Or if the Ball is struck up and he wilfully strikes it again.

Or if in running a Notch the Wicket is struck down by a Throw, or with the Ball in Hand before his Foot, Hand, or Bat is grounded over the Popping Crease; but if the Bail is off, a Stump must be struck out of the Ground by the Ball.

If the striker touches or takes up the Ball before it has come still settled at the Request of the Opposite Party.

Or if the stroke puts his Legs before the Wicket, with a Design to stop the Ball, and actually prevent the Ball from hitting his Wicket by it.

If the Players have stopped each other, he that runs for the Wicket

that is put down is out. If any are out injured, be that has hit the Wicket that is put down is out.

When the Ball has been in the Bowler's or Wicket Keepers Hands, the Strikers need not keep within their Ground, till the Umpire has called Play; but if the Player goes out of his Ground with an Intent to run before the Ball is delivered, the Bowler may put him out.

When the Ball is struck up in the Running Ground between the Wickets, it is lawful for the Strikers to hinder the catching, and may their number strike at nor touch the Ball with their Hands.

If the Ball is struck up the Striker may guard his Wicket, either with his Bat or his Body.

No Single Wicket Striker, if the Striker moves out of his Ground to strike at the Ball, he shall be allowed no Notch for such Notch.

THE WICKET KEEPER.

Shall stand at a reasonable Distance behind the Wicket, and shall not move till the Ball is out of the Bowlers Hand, and shall not by any Noise incommode the Striker, and if his Hands, Knees, Foot or Head be over or before the Wicket, though the Ball touch it, it shall not be out.

THE UMPIRES.

Shall allow Two Minutes for each Man to come in, and Ten between each Innings, when the Umpire shall call Play, the Party refusing to play, shall lose the Match.

They are the sole Judges of all fair and unfair play, and shall determine all Disputes. When a Striker is Out, this is to allow another to come in, and the Person Out, shall have his Hands in any Part of his Innings.

They are not to order a Player out unless appealed to by the Adversaries. But if the Bowlers Foot is not behind the Bowling Crease, when he delivers the Ball the Umpire (unasked) must call no Ball.

If the Strikers run a short Notch, the Umpire must call no Notch.

BETS.

If the Notches of one Player are laid against another, the Bet depends on both Innings unless otherwise specified.

If One Party beats the other in one Innings, the Notches in the first Innings shall determine the Bet.

But if the other Party goes in a second Innings then the Bet must be determined by the Numbers on the Score.

THE END.

FOREWORD

Is it too embarrassing for a cricketer of thirty years' standing, fifteen years of which were spent playing professionally, to admit that he has never read completely the laws governing the game he has played? Moreover, if a snap poll was taken of the 400 or so professional cricketers in England, as well as the many thousands of recreational players, I would lay a very large wager that the vast majority have not done so either. Perhaps this is a pertinent point to ask the question: how relevant are these laws?

Rather like rules of golf, the Laws of Cricket seem occasionally arcane, obtuse even. Nor do they withstand modern scrutiny. Technological advances have recently shown how every bowler thereabouts breaks the law on throwing by straightening his arm to some degree or other. (Hence the amendment to the playing conditions by the ICC that bowlers are allowed fifteen degrees latitude.)

Laws, being laws rather than rules, suggest inflexibility. Yet over time players of all abilities and stature have come to regard some as more important than others. After all, people who regard themselves as law-abiding citizens habitually break the speed limit. So many professional bowlers (and others!)

5

have not been immune over time to artificially altering the state of the ball. Seam picking was as rife in the Lancashire and Cheshire league where I started playing, as it was in the professional game I later joined.

Given that these laws came into being out of a need for something to act as an arbiter between gambling gentlemen, perhaps we should not view them with such reverence. However, let us not be

churlish. Rather like democracy, which is said to be flawed but just about the best flawed arrangement we have, the laws are the best and only reference we cricketers have.

Even now, the crisis following a recent Test match has highlighted to many the chaos that ensues when these laws are dismissed, bypassed, or ignored. Maybe I should get around to reading them after all.

Mike Atherton

Tom Lord

INTRODUCTION

THE TROUBLE WITH CRICKETERS these days is that they've got no respect for the rules. A player can't go out to bat without being subjected to a barrage of crude and derisive comments – all this sledging has clearly got out of hand. And it's not just the sledging: in recent years we've seen aggressive appealing, allegations of match-fixing, ball-tampering, and heaven knows what else. No wonder the guardians of the noble game were moved to add a preface to the latest set of laws, on the edifying theme of 'The Spirit of Cricket'. 'Oh dear, oh dear', as the late Fred Trueman might have ruefully opined (and frequently did). Those fine upstanding fellows who nurtured the game in its infancy must be turning in their graves.

Or perhaps not. Time for a reality check. The art of sledging, for example, might only have acquired its present name more recently but history suggests that this form of gamesmanship – where fielders hurl caustic put-downs at the batsman to upset his concentration – is as old as the game itself. Why else would the original Laws of cricket include a ruling to the effect that the wicketkeeper 'shall not, by any noise, incommode the Striker'.

John Nyren, who dispensed improving advice to young cricketers in the early nineteenth century, warns wicketkeepers against unsettling the batsman 'either by noise, uncalled-for remarks, or unnecessary action'. And sixty-odd years later, the gentleman cricketer Ranjitsinhji wryly observed that a batsman might sometimes be dismissed by being 'talked out', adding that 'Batsmen are quite within their rights in requesting conversational fieldsmen to hold their tongues.'

What about gambling, then? The twenty-first-century ICC Code of Conduct, which prescribes the behaviour expected of players and officials in international cricket, sets out the penalties for anyone who bets on the outcome of games or, worse, gets involved in match-fixing scams. As in many other sports, this is a major concern for today's administrators, and the Hansie Cronje affair of the late 1990s was a dark moment in cricket's recent history. Surely this kind of thing didn't go on in the olden days? *Au contraire.* Betting on games was rife when cricket's earliest laws were enacted. Indeed, a case can be made for saying that the chief stimulus for the original code was the need to regulate the conduct of games in which astonishingly large amounts of gamblers' money were at stake.

Anyone familiar with the writings of Fielding and Smollett or with the engravings of Hogarth will be aware that the English upper classes in the pre-Victorian era were incorrigible gamblers. For aristocrats with a betting addiction, any competitive event would do as a vehicle for gambling, be it prize-fighting, horse racing – or cricket. The history of cricket long pre-dates the first code of laws, but when – as began to happen in the early eighteenth century – sums as high as 1,000 guineas could hang on the outcome of a game, the need for regulation became pressing. Match reports of the period regularly mention the bets riding on the result. Take

this extract from a story in the *St James's Evening Post* of 29 June 1732: 'There were several very considerable wagers laid of the first hands [=innings] which were won by the London gamesters by one notch [=one run].'

Meanwhile, in James Love's poetic description of a match between Kent and All England (*Cricket: An Heroic Poem*, 1744), the narrative moves seamlessly from the cricketing action to the progress of the betting – which was clearly an integral part of the day's entertainment:

> But while the drooping *Play'r* invokes the Gods,
> The busy *Better* calculates his *Odds*,
> Swift round the Plain, in buzzing Murmurs run,
> *I'll hold you Ten to Four*, Kent.—*Done Sir.*—*Done*.

One of the original meanings of the verb 'to draw' was to pull out or withdraw (think of drawing a sword, for example). When a contest was undecided, the money wagered on it was 'withdrawn' and all bets were void (a most unsatisfactory outcome, one imagines). So, for example, a report of a game on Lamb's Conduit Fields, in the *Whitehall Evening Post* of 2 September 1736, notes that the teams scored 23 runs each, 'so they drew stakes'. This probably explains why a game that neither side wins is called a *draw*.

All of which illustrates the central role of gambling in cricket's trajectory, during the early eighteenth century, from a rustic pastime played mainly by children, to an organized sport patronized by the aristocracy and played according to agreed rules.

However, then, as now, the 'it wasn't like this in my day' tendency was on hand to supply an alternative narrative. An early revision of the original Laws, published in 1774, includes a clause for regulating the bets on a game:

> Bets.—If the notches of one player are laid against another, the bet depends on both innings, unless otherwise specified.
>
> If one party beats the other in one innings, the notches in the first innings shall determine the bet.
>
> But if the other party goes in a second time, then the bet must be determined by the number on the score.

Yet in the same year, a jeremiad in the *Chelmsford Chronicle*, unearthed by cricket historian G. B. Buckley, laments that the 'manly' game has been 'perverted from diversion and innocent pastime to excessive gaming and dissipation: Cricket matches are now degenerated into business'. Sound familiar?

In the Beginning

How had all this come about? The earliest incontrovertible evidence for the existence of cricket appears around 1550, but the game was almost certainly played in some form for decades – or, according to some historians, centuries – before that. Vestiges of the game's most ancient form are found in terms that are still in use today: in early cricket, the ball would be literally *bowled* (along the ground) at a tree or tree *stump*. But players must have felt the need for a more portable target, and this led to the use of the movable hurdles used for erecting sheep pens, or of the *wickets* (small gates) by which such pens were entered. Meanwhile, the term *popping crease* harks back to an antique system for scoring runs – probably in use during the seventeenth century – in which a hole was cut in the ground between the stumps

and (to quote John Nyren again) 'in running a notch [= taking a run] the striker was required to put his bat into this hole.' The wicketkeeper, for his part, had to put the ball in this hole in order to run the batsman out. Not surprisingly, with batsman and wicketkeeper competing to 'pop' bat or ball in the hole, there were 'many severe injuries of the hands', so a safer method had to be devised for establishing that a run had been successfully taken. The first attempt involved the batsman touching a stick held by the umpire but this was superseded by the practice still in use today – with the batsman's crease a symbolic vestige of the original 'popping hole'.

But all these changes had already taken place long before the laws of cricket were first codified. The narrative poem *In Certamen Pilae* (written in Latin by William Goldwin in 1706 and translated in 1922 by H. A. Perry, from *The Laws of Cricket* by R. S. Rait Kerr) describes a form of cricket that looks very like the game as it is defined in the earliest laws. There are two umpires and two scorers, a leather ball, and a toss to decide who goes in first. There are four balls to the over, and two sets of wickets, each consisting of

> twin rods that forkèd heads uprear
> with ends set firmly in the green
> . . . and next a milk-white Bail is laid

from fork to fork, whereby is swayed
the dubious issue of the fight

Another verse describes a fielder (the Latin term is *explorator*) taking a catch in the deep – then jubilantly throwing the ball in the air just as any modern player would. At this point in the game's evolution, a run was completed when the batsman touched the umpire's stick, but in most respects this looks like the kind of cricket played throughout the eighteenth century.

From the evidence of this poem, and of contemporary illustrations, it is fair to conclude that the game was already being played according to conventions that were well established and generally accepted, though no doubt allowing for some local variation. This is hardly surprising – there are, after all, contemporary accounts of 'great matches' from 1697 onwards, and this presupposes a degree of regulation (even if this fell short of a standard written code).

The first evidence of anything approximating a set of rules appears in 1727. Two games were to be played in July of that year between teams formed by the Second Duke of Richmond and a Mr Alan Brodrick. A fascinating document found in the Richmond family archives preserves the 'Articles of

Agreement' according to which these games were to be conducted. One of the clauses (Article 10) deals explicitly with the issue of money: 'That each Match shall be for twelve Guineas of each side, between the Duke & Mr Brodrick.'

Another appears to regulate dissent and appealing, by stipulating that there will be two umpires, and that: 'if any of the Gamesters shall speak or give their Opinion on any Point of the Game, they are to be turned out and voided in the Match.' But in deference to the status of the two patrons, it adds that this sanction is 'not to extend to the Duke of Richmond & Mr Brodrick'. Some men, obviously, were more equal than others. As in the game described in the poem of twenty years earlier, runs were completed when the batsman touched a stick held by the umpire: 'The Batt Men, for every One they count, are to touch the Umpire's Stick.'

But it's important to stress that the sixteen Articles in this handwritten document fall a long way short of forming a complete code of laws. This led Colonel Rait Kerr (Secretary of the MCC in the mid-twentieth century and doyen of all matters legislative) to speculate that 'such Articles were used merely to supplement Laws generally accepted for common use'.

The Original Laws of Cricket

On 15 May 1755, a booklet was advertised for sale by the Fleet Street bookseller W. Reeve. Entitled 'The Game at CRICKET, As settled by the Several CRICKET-CLUBS, particularly the STAR and GARTER In PALL-MALL', it contains a complete set of rules that regulate every aspect of the game. A similar code had in fact been published in the November 1752 issue of the *New Universal Magazine*, under the title 'The game at CRICKET, as settled by the CRICKET-CLUB in 1744, and play'd at the ARTILLERY-GROUND, LONDON'.

There are no significant differences between these two sets of Laws, except that the language employed in the later version is more 'modern', with the ball now referred to as 'it' (rather than 'she'), and the antique 'ye' replaced by 'the'. But the 1755 version represents the first unequivocal set of cricket laws issued as a discrete publication, and it is this code – a copy of which is preserved in the MCC library – which is generally seen as embodying 'the original laws of cricket'.

By this time, cricket had become an organized sport. It was played in the city as well as in the country, it involved well-established clubs (rather than just scratch teams put together by wealthy patrons), and – as we have seen – it was often played for very high stakes. These were the conditions in which common practice and generally accepted conventions hardened into a comprehensive set of rules, which were agreed among the leading clubs and applicable to any game played anywhere.

The rules of 1755 are often written in the idiom of the day: the term 'notch', for example, is used in preference to 'run' (which didn't appear for another fifty years or so). The laws in use today are marked by a far greater degree of precision and level of detail, but how far does the game described in those original rules resemble cricket as it is played in the twenty-first century? In some ways, hardly at all. Today's professional

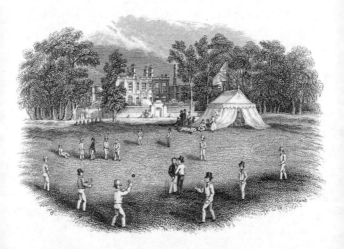

game, with its heavily-armoured batsmen, super-fit acrobatic fielders, and bowlers sending down balls with an overarm action (their pace to be measured by speed guns, their trajectory assessed by Hawk-Eye) would scarcely be recognized by the rustics depicted in eighteenth-century paintings by artists like Francis Hayman, wielding bats shaped more like hockey sticks to defend a two-stump wicket. However, an analysis of the Laws of 1755 suggests these differences are superficial, and shows how much of the modern form of cricket was already in place over 250 years ago. What's remarkable is not the extent to which the rules have changed since the eighteenth century, but the fact that so much of the original code remains essentially intact. When Darrell Hair and Billy Doctrove removed the bails at the Oval in August 2006,

and declared that Pakistan had forfeited the Fourth Test against England by refusing to play, the law they invoked (Law 21 §3 (a)) was not, in its essentials, different from the final clause in the original code of 1755: 'When both Umpires call Play three Times, 'tis at the Peril of giving the Game from them that refuse to play.'

The booklet published in 1755 contains six main sections. The first deals with the dimensions of the pitch, creases, ball, and wicket, and adds that, once the wickets are pitched and the creases cut, 'The Party that wins the Toss-up, may order which Side shall go inn first.' The second section prescribes the 'Laws for the Bowlers'. It specifies the length of an over (four balls) and the conditions in which a delivery can be called as a no-ball, adding that in such cases the ball does not count even if 'the Player be bowl'd out'. The next section, headed 'Laws for the Strikers', lists the various ways in which a batsman can be out. As well as the 'obvious' forms of dismissal, we find that 'hit the ball twice' is already on the statute book, while the equally rare case of 'handled the ball' is covered by the following clause: 'If the Striker touches, or takes up the Ball before it has lain quite still, unless ask'd by the Bowler, or Wicket-Keeper, it's out.'

The fourth section is a something of a ragbag, holding miscellaneous rules about when the ball becomes 'dead' (though the term is not used explicitly) and about what happens if the wicket is struck by the ball but the bail is not dislodged. It includes an interesting sentence indicating that batsmen were allowed – as long as they stayed in their ground – to use their bodies or bats to prevent a fielder from catching the ball. We infer that players were not queuing up to field at bat-pad. A brief fifth section gives 'Laws for the Wicket-keepers', noting that they: 'shall stand at a reasonable Distance behind the Wicket and shall not move till the Ball is out of the Bowler's Hand'.

Nor should any part of the wicketkeeper's body be over or in front of the wicket – a provision which survives (in more elaborate wording, but with the same intent) in Law 40 §3 of the modern code. The sixth and last section, the 'Laws for the Umpires', establishes two enduring features of the umpire's role: first, that the umpire cannot give a batsman out unless appealed to by a member of the fielding side, and secondly that his decision is final. The umpire is: 'the sole Judge of all Nips and Catches; Inns and Outs; good or bad Runs . . . and his Determination shall be absolute'.

Then and Now: Original and Contemporary Codes Compared

The measurements of the pitch, creases, wicket, and ball have changed relatively little in the intervening 250 years. The popping crease, for example, was set at 'Three Feet and Ten Inches' in front of the wicket, as against four feet in today's game. The weight of the ball was to be 'between Five and Six Ounces'; the range has narrowed a little (to 'not less than 5½ ounces and not more than 5¾ ounces'), and the modern code also specifies the ball's circumference. The configuration of the wicket, though, has changed significantly. The older form of wicket (wider than it was high) had been superseded, as Gideon Haigh puts it, by 'flipping ninety degrees for cricket's first set of laws'. The stumps were at this point 22 inches high (their height rose gradually, reaching the present 28 inches in the 1930s), but critically, there were only *two* of them in 1755 (and hence only a single bail). The length of the pitch, however, was set at 22 yards in these laws, and has remained unchanged ever since. John Nyren, writing in 1833, referred to an old manuscript which described how cricket was played when the game was in its infancy. He notes that, 'about 150 years since, it was the custom . . . to pitch the wickets at the same distance asunder, viz.

the twenty-two yards.' This is equivalent to a 'chain', a unit devised in about 1620 by the mathematician Edmund Gunter, for the measurement of plots of land. Nyren's source (now lost) implies that the chain was already the standard length of a cricket pitch as early as 1680.

In 1755, a batsman could be dismissed in seven different ways: bowled, caught, stumped, run out, hit the ball twice, handled the ball, and hit wicket. In modern cricket there are three other ways of getting out, two of which are already alluded to in the earli-

est laws. 'Timed out' isn't actually specified as a mode of dismissal in the original code (indeed, it wasn't formally introduced until 1980), but the umpires are instructed 'To allow Two Minutes for each Man to come inn when one is out'. Within reason, a little bit of 'obstructing the field' seems to have been encouraged (as we saw earlier), and – although the umpires are said to be the 'sole Judges of all Hindrances', there is no evidence that you could lose your wicket for thwarting a catch or a run-out attempt.

What is missing, however, is an lbw rule. The umpires could intervene in the case of a batsman 'standing unfair to strike' (there is no further explanation of what this entailed), but this is as close as the 1755 code gets to prohibiting the batsman from using his legs to keep the ball off the stumps. At first sight, this is a startling omission. But at this point in its evolution, cricket was more of a 'side on' game (like baseball or rounders), played with long curving bats. As Nyren observed, 'with such a bat, the system must have been all for hitting', and – as the low scores of the time suggest – defence of the wicket and occupation of the crease didn't yet add up to a viable strategy. Blocking the ball is unlikely to have been a useful technique in these circumstances, and it wasn't until later in the eighteenth century, when wickets improved and straighter bats began to be used, that the concept of 'leg before wicket' came into play.

In much the same way, several other 'omissions' from these early rules reflect differences in the way the game was played. There is no mention of boundaries, for example: the only way of scoring runs was to run them – and this arrangement continued for

another 100 years or so. W. G. Grace says there were no boundaries at Lord's when he first played there in 1864, and the allowance of four runs for a ball reaching the boundary didn't appear in the laws until twenty years after that.

Nor does the 1755 code have anything to say about the way the ball should be bowled. The

question of what constitutes a legitimate bowling action has exercised the game's legislators for many a year, culminating (for the time being, at least) in a dense fourteen-page ruling published by the International Cricket Council (ICC) in 2006. In highly technical language ('hyperextension angle: the angle between the longitudinal axis of the upper arm and forearm, in the sagittal plane') these new regulations provide for the appointment of a panel of 'human movement specialists', and describe elaborate protocols for analysing the movements of any bowler with a suspect action. The objective is to harness the science of biomechanics in order to establish clear criteria for judging whether a delivery is legal, or whether the ball has been 'thrown' rather than bowled. The document concludes with a description of the 'acceptable level of elbow extension', ruling that 'this should be set at a maximum of 15 degrees.' But some observers of the game have made up their minds that certain players are 'chuckers', and whether they will be appeased by these scientific convolutions is anybody's guess.

Back in 1755, though, life was a good deal simpler. The bitter controversies of the nineteenth century, as good old-fashioned bowling (with an underarm action) was replaced first by 'roundarm' and later by 'overarm', were still some way off. Apart from specify-

ing the position of the bowler's foot ('If he delivers the Ball, with his hinder Foot over the Bowling-Crease, the Umpire shall call no Ball'), the original rules say nothing about how the ball should be delivered. From this we infer that it simply wasn't an issue. The standard repertoire at this point included daisy-cutters, lobs, and the newly emerging 'length ball' (which bounced once, from what we would now call a 'good length', before reaching the batsman) – all bowled with an underarm action. And that, for the time being, was that.

Interestingly, the *size* of a cricket team isn't specified in the laws till as late as 1884. In early match reports, we find teams of anything from three to thirty-three players, the latter in a game of 1797, between '11 of All England and 33 of Norfolk'. The idea in such cases was to set up a more balanced contest by packing the weaker side with extra players – though in this particular match the Norfolk men somehow contrived to lose by an innings. But the evidence suggests that, from a very early stage, a team of eleven players was in fact the norm. H. S. Altham's classic *History of Cricket* reproduces an engraving from about 1740, in which we can clearly see eleven men on the fielding side. Earlier still, the *Foreign Post* reports on a 'great match at Cricket' played in Sussex in July 1697. The names of the opposing teams are not recorded, but we are told that 'they were eleven of a side'. It's reasonable to see a Darwinian process at work here, with eleven gradually establishing itself as the perfect number. Every selector (whether official or of the 'armchair' variety) knows that a team of this size is just large enough to give its captain a range of options (in the field or when batting), but just small enough to pose interesting tactical challenges: we'd like to bring in a spinner, but that'll weaken our fast-bowling attack, and what if the wicket doesn't turn? This wicket is perfect for bowler X – but he's a duffer with the bat, so what happens if there's a top-order collapse? We *have* to get a result in this game – a draw is no use to us – so which configuration is most likely to achieve this? And so, endlessly, on. From the available evidence, it looks as if the evolutionary process had already run its course by 1755, and – even if there is no explicit reference here to team size – most games of cricket were being contested by teams of eleven players when the original laws were formulated.

What Happened Next . . .

NEW
ARTICLES
OF THE
GAME OF CRICKET,
As settled and revised at the
STAR and GARTER, *Pall-Mall*,
FEBRUARY the 25th, 1774;
BY A COMMITTEE OF NOBLEMEN
AND GENTLEMEN OF KENT, &c.

Embellished with a neat emblematical Representation of the Game.

MAIDSTONE:
PRINTED AND SOLD BY J. BLAKE; SOLD ALSO BY ALL THE BOOKSELLERS, AND THE PERSONS WHO SELL CRICKET BATS, BALLS, &c.

A revised edition of the original laws appeared in 1774, this one undertaken by a committee representing London and the cricket-playing counties of south-east England. Further revisions followed at intervals of anything from twelve to sixty-odd years. The laws in use today were published in 2000, but even these have been supplemented by a steady stream of 'codes of conduct', 'playing conditions', and other directives issued

by the ICC and local governing bodies – including the aforementioned treatise on hyperextension angles. What were the factors that led to these changes?

Part of the motivation for adding new laws (or amending existing ones) is a simple concern to improve the game – to maintain the delicate balance between bat and ball (so that neither becomes dominant), and to make the cricket fairer for players and more entertaining for spectators. The rules governing lbws and no-balls, for example, have been tweaked several times in an effort to make them more equitable. Thus in 1937, the lbw law – which at first dealt only with balls pitching on a line between the two sets of stumps – was extended to include the case of a ball that pitched outside off but went on to hit the batsman standing 'between wicket and wicket'. But canny players soon worked out a way of circumventing this: by moving the front foot towards the off side, the batsman could 'pad up' to a ball pitching outside off-stump but heading towards the wicket. If the ball was not 'between wicket and wicket' when it hit your pad, you couldn't be out. In an England–West Indies Test in 1957, Colin Cowdrey and Peter May notoriously employed this tactic to thwart the opposition's spinners – and put on 411 runs in the process. This may have been good for England's chances, but it was excruciatingly tedious for anyone watching. A further change to the rules (in 1970) seems to have been expressly designed to combat this kind of negative batting. Under this revised version (still in place today), the batsman could be out to a ball pitching outside off *and* hitting the batsman outside off – provided the umpire judged that the batsman wasn't trying to hit the ball (and, of course, that the ball would have hit the stumps if it hadn't been blocked). Thus do the rules evolve to make the game fairer and to guard the interests of the paying public.

Much earlier, but in a similar spirit, a third stump had been added after Kent player 'Lumpy' Stevens bowled three deliveries right through the gap in John Small's wicket, in a game against Hambledon in 1775. As a contemporary noted, 'it was considered to be a hard thing upon the bowler that his straightest balls should be thus sacrificed.' Kent's star bowler was the victim of his own success, and to prevent this happening again, the wicket acquired its middle stump (and in due course, a second bail). The increase in the length of an over (from four balls to five in 1889, and from five to six in 1900) was driven not so much by the pursuit of equity as by the opportunities this offered the bowler for developing a tactical plan. There had been a gradual improvement in playing surfaces during the nineteenth century, and batting techniques had improved as a consequence, leading to higher-scoring games. A longer over helped to redress the balance. Adjustments like this continue to be made – think for example of the fielding restrictions and Powerplay rules introduced to add variation and excitement to the one-day game.

Developments in technology have been another driver of legislative change. With modern TV cameras, it became possible for a 'third umpire' to use replays in order to adjudicate on run-outs, stumpings, and other close calls that the on-field umpires might be less well-placed to rule on. But although a third umpire has been employed in international cricket since 1993, the debate on the appropriate role of technology is still very much alive. Some would maintain the historic principle that the umpires should be 'the sole Judges of all Outs and Inns', while others argue that it makes sense to use any technical aid that will help bring a fair decision – and will incidentally protect umpires from the inevitable fall-out of a bad call which is immediately displayed on a huge screen. But even in the eighteenth century, emerging technologies had their impact. The design of the bat underwent significant changes in the 1760s, becoming straighter, wider, and generally much more like its modern self. This led to the refinement of batting techniques as players sought to defend their wickets rather than just slogging away. The introduction of an lbw rule, in the first revision of the Laws in 1774, can be seen as a direct consequence. From now on, the batsman was out if he: 'puts his leg before the wicket with a design to stop the ball, and actually prevents the ball from hitting his wicket by it'.

New technology, new techniques, and hence new rules. But there's a fine line between adapting your game to changing circumstances, and exploiting inadequacies in the rules for your own benefit. The history of cricket's laws provides abundant evidence of a back-and-forth process in which players bend the rules to their advantage until the legislators plug the relevant loophole. Just as clever tax lawyers will pore over fiscal regulations to spot any weakness that might benefit their clients, cricketers have, for centuries, shown themselves adept at various forms of gamesmanship. Even in the code of 1755, the wording of several clauses hints at sharp practice. Fielders were not above getting in the way of a batsman taking a run, so the law allows the umpires to order a run to be scored 'if either of the Strikers is cross'd in his running Ground, designedly'. It's a good rule of thumb that a law explicitly forbidding a certain action has probably come into being because this action is prevalent and the legislators want to discourage it. So when the original Laws state that the umpires are to be the arbiters 'of all fair and unfair Play; of all frivolous Delays; of all Hurts, whether real or pretended', we can fairly surmise that 'pushing the boundaries' was as pervasive in the eighteenth century as it is today. Time-wasting, feigning injury, even sledging – it's all there.

The laws said nothing about the dimensions of the bat until 1771, when – in a splendid example of gamesmanship – a certain Mr White of Reigate came in to bat against Hambledon, with a bat which 'being the width of the stumps, effectually defended his wicket from the bowler'. An immediate amendment was drafted by the Hambledon club to close this loophole, limiting the width of the bat to 4¼ inches. This ruling was incorporated into the revised code of 1774 – and the width of the bat hasn't changed since. It was not until two centuries later that the laws had anything to say about the *composition* of the bat, which was simply assumed to be wood. Assumed, that is, until Dennis Lillee's experiments with an aluminium bat in the 1979–80 Ashes series. Shortly afterwards, a new clause appeared

in the laws, stating rather huffily that 'the blade of the bat shall be made of wood'. White of Reigate would have understood exactly what Lillee was up to.

In similar fashion, the art of bowling developed during the nineteenth century, as bowlers tested the laws by experimenting with new modes of delivery (first roundarm, then overarm). The game's lawmakers initially responded by outlawing any change but eventually capitulated when it became clear that the tide was unstoppable. Various rearguard actions were mounted, but the effort was finally abandoned in 1864. A new ruling in that year, tersely stating that 'The ball must be bowled,' effectively lifted the embargo on the more modern bowling actions which soon gained the ascendancy. But, inevitably, the wording of this clause proved in the end to be just a little too permissive. In 1981, Australian bowler Trevor Chappell bowled an underarm daisy-cutter in the final over of a one-day international – making it impossible for New Zealand to score the six they needed to win the game. And this explains the modern ruling that 'Underarm bowling shall not be permitted except by special agreement before the match' (Law 24 §1 (a)).

Finally, no discussion of the rules (and of players' attempts to circumvent them) would be complete without some mention of ball-tampering. Even in

1755, the drafters of the original laws had enjoined the umpires to 'mark the Ball, that it may not be changed'. Much later, bowlers realized that altering the condition of the ball could affect its movement in flight and off the pitch. This might just be a case of allowing one side of the ball to become rougher with wear, while keeping the other side smooth and shiny by the familiar expedient of rubbing it on your trousers. Picking the seam, as Michael Atherton observes in his foreword, has been rife in the game for years, and was first outlawed in the code of 1947. But this is where we enter a grey area. Most fair-minded people would agree that gouging the ball's surface with a metal bottle-cap, as one well-known player admitted to doing in the 1990s, is a step too far. But what about 'accidentally' scraping the ball on the ground, as you field it, in order to roughen one of its surfaces? Or applying the sweat of your brow, with the aim of making one side of the ball heavier than the other and so encouraging it to swing in flight? It all depends. The current rules on 'fair and unfair play' make valiant efforts to define what is and is not permissible, and are backed up by the ICC's Code of Conduct. But the truth is that enterprising cricketers, with an eye to gaining advantage by bending the rules, will always be one step ahead.

Cricket is now a global sport, regulated not only by its laws but by the various 'codes of practice', 'playing conditions', and other directives issued by the ICC or its local outposts. The large sums wagered on games 250 years ago are dwarfed by today's multi-million-pound media contracts and sponsorship deals. With so much at stake, the regulatory system is, inevitably, more complex and more rigorous than anything that came before. The Duckworth/Lewis rules alone (for calculating required targets in rain-affected matches) run to fifteen pages and come with their own software. For all that, the game we watch today retains the essential ethos of eighteenth-century cricket. Then as now, gamesmanship was part of the mix, as players looked for loopholes and tested the boundaries to see what they could get away with. But then as now, they enjoyed their cricket and played it in a spirit of honest competition. What started, many centuries ago, as a rural pastime in the south of England has become an international sporting phenomenon. And the vital first steps in this transformation were taken when the original laws of cricket were written down in 1755.

THE 1744 CODE
OF THE LAWS OF
CRICKET

of a *ase' cut 3 feet 10 Inches*
ing *Creases must be cut in a*
om *mp if stumps must be 22In*
op- *Ball must weigh between*
Cre- *are both pitchd, & all if cre*

THE GAME OF CRICKET AS SETTLED BY
Ye CRICKET CLUB AT Ye STAR AND GARTER
IN PALL MALL.

The pitching ye first Wicket is to be determined by ye cast of a piece of Money. When ye first Wicket is pitched and ye popping Crease Cut which must be exactly 3 Foot 10 Inches from ye Wicket ye Other Wicket is to be pitched directly opposite at 22 yards distance and ye other popping crease cut 3 Foot 10 Inches before it. The Bowling Creases must be cut in a direct line from each stump. The Stumps must be 22 Inches long and ye Bail 6 Inches. The Ball must weigh between 5 and 6 Ounces. When ye Wickets are both pitched and all ye Creases Cut The Party that wins the toss up may order which side shall go in first at his Option.

Laws for Ye Bowlers 4 Balls and Over.

The Bowler must deliver ye Ball with one foot behind ye Crease even with ye Wicket and When he has Bowled one Ball or more shall Bowl to ye number 4 before he Changes Wickets and he Shall Change but once in ye Same Innings. He may order ye Player that is in at his wicket to Stand on which side of it he Pleases at a reasonable distance. If he delivers ye Ball with his hinder foot over ye Bowling crease ye Umpire Shall Call no Ball though she be Struck or ye Player bowled out Which he shall do without being asked and no Person shall have any right to ask him.

Laws for Ye Strikers, or those that are in.

If ye Wicket is Bowled down its out. If he Strikes or treads down or falls himself upon ye wicket in Striking (but not in over running) its out. A Stroke or Nip over or under his Batt or upon his hands (but not arms) if ye Ball be held before She touches ye Ground though She be hugged to the Body its out. If in Striking both his feet are over ye popping crease his Wicket put down except his Batt is down within its out. If he runs out of his Ground to hinder a Catch its out. If a Ball is nipped up and he Strikes her again Wilfully before she comes to ye Wicket its out. If ye Players have Crossed each other he that runs for ye Wicket that is put down is out. If they are not Crossed he that returns is out. If in running a Notch ye Wicket is struck down by a Throw before his Foot Hand or Batt is over ye Popping crease or a Stump hit by ye Ball though ye Bail was down its out. But if ye Bail is down before he that catches ye Ball must strike a Stump out of ye Ground Ball in Hand then its out. If ye Striker touches or takes up ye Ball before she is lain quite still unless asked by ye Bowler or Wicket keeper its out.

ully before she comes to the Wick
...avers have crost'd each other, be
Wicket that is put down, is out
...crost'd, he that retu... ...out. If
...Notch, if Wicket is struck down by...

Batt Foot or Hand over ye Crease.

When ye Ball has been in Hand by one of ye Keepers or Stoppers and ye Player has been at home He may go where he pleases till ye next Ball is bowled. If Either of ye Strikers is crossed in his running Ground designedly, which design must be determined by the Umpires. NB The Umpires may order that notch to be Scored. When ye Ball is hit up either of ye strikers may hinder ye catch in his running Ground or if She is hit directly across ye Wickets ye Other Player may place his Body any where within ye Swing of his Batt so as to hinder ye Bowler from catching her, but he must neither Strike at her nor touch her with his hands. If a striker nips a Ball up just before him he may fall before his Wicket, or pop down his Batt before She comes to it to save it. The Bail hanging on one stump though ye Ball hit ye Wicket its not out.

when what Time they think p
hat it on again—In case of a
Ins, of are to allow another to
rts wb to come in again But a
allow Man to play, on either Sic

Laws for Wicket Keepers.

The Wicket Keepers shall stand at reasonable distance behind ye Wicket and shall not move till ye Ball is out of ye Bowler's Hands and shall not by any noise incommode ye Striker and if his hands knees foot or head be over or before his Wicket though the Ball hit, it shall not be out.

Laws for ye Umpires.

To allow 2 Minutes for each man to come in when one is out, and 10 Minutes between Each Hand To mark ye Ball that it may not be changed. They are sole judges of all outs and ins, of all fair and unfair Play or frivolous delays, of all hurts whether real or pretended and are discretionally to allow what time they think Proper before ye Game goes on again. In case of a real hurt to a Striker they are to allow another

er before y Game goes ...sole J...
...l Hurt to a Striker, they runni...
...me in, & y Person hurt ...nce...
...not to allow a fresh ___ ...to orde...
...n any Account They are ...of y Pla...

to come in and the Person hurt to come in again But
are not to allow a fresh Man to Play on either side on
any Account. They are sole judges of all hindrances,
crossing ye Players in running and Standing unfair to
Strike and in case of hindrance may order a Notch to
be Scored. They are not to order any man out unless
appealed to by one of ye Players. These Laws are to ye
Umpires Jointly. Each Umpire is ye Sole Judge of all
Nips and Catches Ins and outs good or bad runs at
his own Wicket and his determination shall be absolute and he shall not be changed for another Umpire
without ye Consent of both Sides. When ye 4 Balls are
Bowled he is to call over. These Laws are Separately.
When both Umpires shall call Play 3 Times 'tis at ye
Peril of giving ye Game from them that refuse Play.

THE 1755 CODE
OF THE LAWS OF
CRICKET

THE

ARTICLES

OF THE

GAME

OF

CRICKET,

As ſettled by the ſeveral

CRICKET-CLUBS,

Particularly that of the

STAR and GARTER,
In PALL-MALL.

(With a neat COPPER PLATE of the
Repreſentation of the Game.)

THE GAME AT CRICKET.

The Pitching the first Wicket is to be determined by the Toss of a Piece of Money. When the first Wicket is pitch'd, and the Popping-Crease cut, which must be exactly Three Feet Ten Inches from the Wicket, the other Wicket is to be pitch'd directly opposite, at Twenty-Two Yards Distance, and the other Popping-Crease cut Three Feet and Ten Inches before it.

The Bowling-Creases must be cut in a direct Line from each Stump.

The Stumps must be Twenty-Two Inches long, and the Bail Six Inches.

The Ball must weigh between Five & Six Ounces.

When the Wickets are both pitch'd, and all the Creases cut, the Party that wins the Toss-up, may order which Side shall go inn first, at his Option.

LAWS FOR THE BOWLERS.

Four Balls and Over.

The Bowler must deliver the Ball, with one Foot behind the Crease, even with the Wicket; and when he has bowl'd one Ball, or more, shall bowl to the Number of Four before

he changes wickets, and he shall change but once in the same Innings.

He may order the Player that is inn at his Wicket, to stand on which Side of it he pleases, at a reasonable Distance.

If he delivers the Ball, with his hinder Foot over the Bowling-Crease, the Umpire shall call no Ball, tho' it be struck, or the Player be bowl'd out; which he shall do without being ask'd, and no Person shall have any Right to question him.

LAWS FOR THE STRIKERS, or THOSE that are INN.

If the Wicket is bowl'd down, it's out.

If he strikes, or treads down, or falls himself upon his Wicket in striking (but not in over-running) it's out. A Stroke, or Nip, over or under his Bat, or upon his Hands (but not Arms) if the Ball be held before it touches the Ground, though it be hugg'd to the Body, it's out.

If in striking, both his Feet are over the Popping-Crease, and his Wicket put down, except his Bat is down within, it's out.

If he runs out of his Ground to hinder a Catch, it's out.

If a Ball is nipp'd up, and he strikes it again wilfully, before it came to the Wicket, it's out.

If the Players have cross'd each other, he that runs for the Wicket that is put down, is out: If they are not crossed, he that returns is out.

If in running a Notch, the Wicket is struck down by a Throw, before his Foot, Hand, or Bat is over the Popping-Crease, or a Stump hit by the Ball, though the Bail was down, it's out.

But if the Bail is down before, he that catches the Ball must strike a Stump out of the Ground, Ball in Hand, or else it's not out.

If the Striker touches, or takes up the Ball before it has lain quite still, unless ask'd by the Bowler, or Wicket-Keeper, it's out.

BAT, FOOT or HAND, over the CREASE.

When the Ball has been in Hand by one of the Keepers, or Stoppers, and the Player has been at Home, he may go where he pleases till the next Ball is bowl'd.

If either of the Strikers is crossed, in his running Ground, designedly, the same must be determined by the Umpires.

N.B. The Umpires may order that Notch to be scored.

When the Ball is hit up, either of the Strikers may hinder the Catch in his running Ground; or if it is hit directly across the Wickets, the other player may place his Body anywhere within the Swing of the Bat so as to hinder the Bowler from catching it; but he must neither strike at it, nor touch it with his Hands.

If a Striker nips a Ball up just before him, he may fall before his Wicket, or pop down his Bat, before it comes to the Wicket, to save it.

The Bail hanging on one Stump, though the Ball hit the Wicket, it's not out.

LAWS for the WICKET-KEEPERS.

The Wicket-Keepers shall stand at a reasonable Distance behind the Wicket, and shall not move till the Ball is out of the Bowler's Hand, and shall not, by

any Noise, incommode the Striker; and if his Hands, Knees, Foot, or Head, be over, or before the Wicket, though the Ball hit it, it shall not be out.

LAWS for the UMPIRES.

To allow Two Minutes for each Man to come inn when one is out, and Ten Minutes between each Hand.

To mark the Ball that it may not be changed.

They are sole Judges of all Outs and Inns; of all fair or unfair Play; of all frivolous Delays; of all Hurts, whether real or pretended, and are discretionally to allow what Time they think proper before the Game goes on again.

In case of a real Hurt to a Striker, they are to allow another to come inn, and the Person hurt to come inn again; but are not to allow a fresh Man to play, on either Side, on any Account.

They are sole Judges of all Hindrances; crossing the Players in running, and standing unfair to strike, and in Case of Hindrance may order a Notch to be scor'd.

They are not to order any Man out, unless appealed to by one of the Players.

These Laws are to the Umpires jointly.

Each Umpire is the sole Judge of all Nips and Catches; Inns and Outs; good or bad Runs, at his own Wicket, and his Determination shall be absolute; and he shall not be changed for another Umpire, without the Consent of both Sides.

When the four Balls are bowl'd, he is to call over.

These Laws are separately.

When both Umpires call Play three Times, 'tis at the Peril of giving the Game from them that refuse to Play.